M000298572

Pro Nobis: Christ's saving work —
Scripture Readings and Patristic Meditations for Easter Week
Selected and Edited by Michael A.G. Haykin

© 2021 by Michael A.G. Haykin

Published by: H&E Publishing, Peterbourough, Ontario
www.hesedandemet.com

Cover painting: *Christ's Appearance to Mary Magdalene after the Resurrection*, 1835 by Alexander Andreyevich Ivanov (1806–1858)

Design and layout: Dustin Benge

Paperback ISBN: 978-1-77484-011-5
Ebook ISBN: 978-1-77484-012-2

First edition, 2021

PRO NOBIS: CHRIST'S SAVING WORK

*Scripture Readings and Patristic Meditations
for Easter Week*

Selected & Edited by
MICHAEL A.G. HAYKIN

H&E
Publishing

CONTENTS

Introduction   7

1   Palm Sunday   11

2   Monday   17

3   Tuesday   23

4   Wednesday   29

5   Thursday   35

6   Good Friday   41

7   Saturday   47

8   Easter Sunday   53

Glossary of Authors   61

INTRODUCTION

Michael A.G. Haykin

Prayerful meditation on the inspired and infallible Word of God should always first lead to a deeper and richer discovery of who God—the Father and the Son and the Holy Spirit—is and what he has done in creation and history. Further, this should lead to a response on our part in prayer and then in deed.

This small devotional consists, first of all, of Scriptures that are focused on the events of Easter Week that relate to the death and resurrection of Christ—the saving work of Christ *pro nobis* (a Latin phrase that means "for us"). These Scriptures are meant to help us revisit what should be utterly foundational for our Christian life, namely, the propitiatory death and bodily resurrection of Jesus Christ. This reflection on what Christ has done *pro nobis* should also lead to a renewed commitment to his service and to the promotion of his kingdom of love.

The writers of the Ancient Church[1]

Accompanying these Scriptures are words and texts from the earliest disciples of Christ—pastors, theologians, and authors from the Ancient Church (from the first century to the ninth century)—who thought long and hard about the events of this most important of all weeks. For all of these writers, these events of Easter Week were utterly central to the meaning of their lives.

Some of these men, like Tertullian and Origen, as well as the author of the *Letter to Diognetus*, experienced persecution from a hostile Roman Imperium for affirming the lordship and unique deity of Christ, as well as his resurrection. In fact, the Alexandrian Bible scholar Origen, who had some ideas that later Christians found unacceptable, felt the full fury of the Roman state when he was arrested in an empire-wide persecution in 250 and tortured so as to deny Christ. Origen did not succumb, and he emerged from prison a broken man physically. He subsequently died as a result of the torture. As he once said, "I wish to be a man of the Church, not the founder of heresy; I want to be named with Christ's name and bear

---

[1] At the back of this devotional, there is a glossary of the writers whose works are cited in this booklet.

the name which is blessed on earth."[2]

Others—such as Athanasius and Hilary of Poitiers, Basil of Caesarea and John Chrysostom—lived in the fourth century when professing Christians held the reins of political power. Christianity had become a legal religion at the beginning of that century and by its close it was the state religion of the Roman Empire. Nonetheless these men had to struggle against the heresy of Arianism, which denied the full deity of Christ and that of the Holy Spirit, as well as to contend with Arian political rulers who sought to enforce their theology upon the churches. Whilst their Arian opponents did not deny the saving events of Easter Week, Athanasius and Basil—as well as the other fourth- and fifth-century authors whose works are cited here— knew from Scripture that if the One who died on the cross was not fully God, their salvation was totally undermined.

Finally, two of the authors cited here—John of Damascus and Timothy of Baghdad—lived under the rule of the Muslims who had conquered most of the Middle East in the seventh century. The Muslim holy book, the Qur'an, denied the deity of Christ, as well as his crucifixion and resurrection. John of Damascus and Timothy were both apologists to Islam and thus the cross and the resurrection were vital matters of doctrine and spirituality for them.

---

[2] Origen, *Homily of Luke* 16.

Reading this devotional & a prayer

The Scripture passages and the readings from the writers of the Ancient Church in this devotional are meant to be read day by day during Easter Week from Palm Sunday to Easter Sunday. As you read these texts, meditate on what Christ has done for us, *pro nobis*, and for our walk with God's people in his Church.

After a most trying year, may our walk together in this year's Easter Week be a time of sweet refreshment, genuine renewal, and true repentance from the presence of the Lord Jesus.

Michael A.G. Haykin
Dundas, Ontario.[3]

---

[3] The basis for this devotional was one that I drew up for the celebration of Easter Week, 1980, at Wycliffe College, the University of Toronto, where I was doing my doctoral studies at the time. It was entitled *Meditations for the Refreshment of the Spirit*. I am grateful to Baiyu Andrew Song for digitizing that text, which I have thoroughly revised and reworked into a brand-new booklet, along with a completely new introduction that I have added. Thanks also to Baiyu for drawing up a good portion of the glossary of names. I am also indebted to Dr. Dustin Benge for doing the layout and design of the present booklet, and for Chance Faulkner in the supervision of its publication.

PALM SUNDAY

⁹ Rejoice greatly, O daughter of Zion! Shout aloud, O daughter of Jerusalem! Behold, your king is coming to you; righteous and having salvation is he, humble and mounted on a donkey, on a colt, the foal of a donkey. ¹⁰ I will cut off the chariot from Ephraim and the war horse from Jerusalem; and the battle bow shall be cut off, and he shall speak peace to the nations; his rule shall be from sea to sea, and from the River to the ends of the earth.

¹ Now when they drew near to Jerusalem and came to

Bethphage, to the Mount of Olives, then Jesus sent two disciples, ² saying to them, "Go into the village in front of you, and immediately you will find a donkey tied, and a colt with her. Untie them and bring them to me. ³ If anyone says anything to you, you shall say, 'The Lord needs them,' and he will send them at once." ⁴ This took place to fulfill what was spoken by the prophet, saying,

> "Say to the daughter of Zion, 'Behold, your king is coming to you, humble, and mounted on a donkey, on a colt, the foal of a beast of burden.'"

⁶ The disciples went and did as Jesus had directed them. ⁷ They brought the donkey and the colt and put on them their cloaks, and he sat on them. ⁸ Most of the crowd spread their cloaks on the road, and others cut branches from the trees and spread them on the road. ⁹ And the crowds that went before him and that followed him were shouting, "Hosanna to the Son of David! Blessed is he who comes in the name of the Lord! Hosanna in the highest!" ¹⁰ And when he entered Jerusalem, the whole city was stirred up, saying, "Who is this?" ¹¹ And the crowds said, "This is the prophet Jesus, from Nazareth of Galilee."

¹² And Jesus entered the temple and drove out all who sold and bought in the temple, and he overturned the tables of the money-changers and the seats of those who sold pigeons. ¹³ He said to them, "It is written, 'My house

shall be called a house of prayer,' but you make it a den of robbers."

¹⁴ And the blind and the lame came to him in the temple, and he healed them. ¹⁵ But when the chief priests and the scribes saw the wonderful things that he did, and the children crying out in the temple, "Hosanna to the Son of David!" they were indignant, ¹⁶ and they said to him, "Do you hear what these are saying?" And Jesus said to them, "Yes; have you never read,

"'Out of the mouth of infants and nursing babies you have prepared praise'?"

¹⁷ And leaving them, he went out of the city to Bethany and lodged there.

MEDITATION:

> All glory, laud, and honour
> To thee, Redeemer, King!
> To whom the lips of children
> Made sweet hosannas ring.
>
> Thou art the King of Israel
> Thou David's Royal Son,
> Who in the Lord's name comest,
> The King and Blessèd One.

The company of angels
Is praising thee on high,
And mortal men, and all things
Created make reply.

The people of the Hebrews
With palms before thee went
Our praise and prayers and anthems
Before thee we present.

To thee before thy passion
They sang their hymns of praise;
To thee now high exalted
Our melody we raise.

Thou didst accept their praises;
Accept the praise we bring,
Who in all good delightest,
Thou good and gracious King.

(Theodulf of Orléans)

NOTES

NOTES

MONDAY

[5] You know that he appeared in order to take away sins, and in him there is no sin.

READING:

Christ is the Word from God and a man from Mary, and … as the Word of God he is the Lord of everything, and as a man he did not commit any sin …, and if he who is the Lord of everything and a creator is not in need, and he who is not a sinner is pure, it follows that Jesus Christ worshipped and prayed to God neither as one in need nor as a sinner, but he worshipped and prayed in order to teach worship and prayer to his disciples and through them to every human being.

The disciples would not have yielded to his teaching, if he had not put it into practice in his own person. There is no creature that has not sinned except Jesus Christ, the Word of God, and he is the only created being who in his own humanity appeared above the dirt of sin. As he was baptized without having any need of baptism, and as he died on the cross but not because of his own sin, so also he gave himself to worship and prayer not for his own sake but in order to impart their knowledge to his disciples.

(Timothy of Baghdad, *Apology for Christianity*)

READING: 1 CORINTHIANS 5:6–8

[6] Your boasting is not good. Do you not know that a little leaven leavens the whole lump? [7] Cleanse out the old leaven that you may be a new lump, as you really are unleavened. For Christ, our Passover lamb, has been sacrificed. [8] Let us therefore celebrate the festival, not with the old leaven, the leaven of malice and evil, but with the unleavened bread of sincerity and truth.

MEDITATION:

If there is joy in heaven over one sinner who repents [Luke 15:7], what must there be over the abolition of sin and the resurrection of the dead? Oh, what a feast and how great the gladness in heaven! How must all its [angelic] hosts joy and exult, as they rejoice and watch in our assemblies … that … are held at Easter?

(Athanasius, *Festal Epistles* 6.10)

READING: 1 PETER 1:3–9

³ Blessed be the God and Father of our Lord Jesus Christ! According to his great mercy, he has caused us to be born again to a living hope through the resurrection of Jesus Christ from the dead, ⁴ to an inheritance that is imperishable, undefiled, and unfading, kept in heaven for you, ⁵ who by God's power are being guarded through faith for a salvation ready to be revealed in the last time. ⁶ In this you rejoice, though now for a little while, if necessary, you have been grieved by various trials, ⁷ so that the tested genuineness of your faith—more precious than gold that perishes though it is tested by fire—may be found to result in praise and glory and honor at the revelation of Jesus Christ. ⁸ Though you have not seen him, you love him. Though you do not now see him, you believe in him and rejoice with joy that is inexpressible and filled with glory, ⁹ obtaining the outcome of your faith, the salvation of your souls.

MEDITATION:

The Lord descended so that he might save sinners, raise up the dead, bring new life to those wounded by death, and enlighten those who lay in darkness. The Lord truly came and called us to be God's adopted children, to enter into a holy city, ever at peace, to possess a life that will endure forever, to share an incorruptible glory.

(Macarius, *Homily* 11.15)

NOTES

NOTES

TUESDAY

⁶ If we say we have fellowship with him while we walk in darkness, we lie and do not practice the truth. ⁷ But if we walk in the light, as he is in the light, we have fellowship with one another, and the blood of Jesus his Son cleanses us from all sin.

MEDITATION:

This blood [of Jesus] is the salvation of our souls; by it the soul is cleansed; by it, it is beautified; by it, it is inflamed. It makes our intellect brighter than fire; it renders our soul more radiant than gold. This blood has been poured forth and has opened the way to heaven.

> (John Chrysostom, *Homilies on the Gospel of St. John* 46)

READING: LUKE 22:39–44

[39] And he came out and went, as was his custom, to the Mount of Olives, and the disciples followed him. [40] And when he came to the place, he said to them, "Pray that you may not enter into temptation." [41] And he withdrew from them about a stone's throw, and knelt down and prayed, [42] saying, "Father, if you are willing, remove this cup from me. Nevertheless, not my will, but yours, be done." [43] And there appeared to him an angel from heaven, strengthening him. [44] And being in agony he prayed more earnestly; and his sweat became like great drops of blood falling down to the ground.

MEDITATION:

Our Lord praying with a bloody sweat represented the martyrdoms which should flow from his whole body, which is the Church.

> (Augustine, cited in *Catena aurea*)

READING: JOHN 19:2

[2] And the soldiers twisted together a crown of thorns and

put it on his head and arrayed him in a purple robe.

MEDITATION:

A crown of thorns, it is written, was set upon him. … If I may disclose to you, however, the heart of a mystery: it was appropriate that he who came to remove the sins of the world should at the same time release the earth from the curses inflicted on it when the first-formed man sinned, and it received the sentence of transgression in the Lord's words, "Cursed is the ground for your sake; … thorns and thistles it shall bring forth for you" [Genesis 3:17–18]. Jesus was therefore crowned with thorns in order that the primordial sentence of condemnation might be remitted.

(Rufinus, *A Commentary on the Apostles' Creed* 22)

NOTES

NOTES

WEDNESDAY

³² And they went to a place called Gethsemane. And he said to his disciples, "Sit here while I pray." ³³ And he took with him Peter and James and John, and began to be greatly distressed and troubled. ³⁴ And he said to them, "My soul is very sorrowful, even to death. Remain here and watch." ³⁵ And going a little farther, he fell on the ground and prayed that, if it were possible, the hour might pass from him. ³⁶ And he said, "Abba, Father, all things are possible for you. Remove this cup from me. Yet not what I will, but what you will." ³⁷ And he came and found them sleeping, and he said to Peter, "Simon, are you asleep? Could you not watch one hour? ³⁸ Watch and pray that you may not

enter into temptation. The spirit indeed is willing, but the flesh is weak." [39] And again he went away and prayed, saying the same words. [40] And again he came and found them sleeping, for their eyes were very heavy, and they did not know what to answer him.

MEDITATION:

I marvel at myself, beloved, how I daily default, and daily do repent. I build up for an hour, and an hour overthrows what I have built. At evening I say, "Tomorrow I shall repent," but when morning comes, joyous I waste the day. Again, at evening I say, "I shall keep vigil all night, and I shall entreat the Lord with tears, to have mercy on my sins," but when night has come, I am full of sleep. … Have mercy upon me, you who are alone without sin, and save me, who alone is pitiful and kind, for besides you, the Father most blessed, and your only begotten Son who became flesh for us, and the Holy Spirit who gives life to all things, I know no other and believe in no other. … Holy Lord, I beseech you, bring me into your kingdom, and deign to bless me with all that have found grace before you, for with you is magnificence, adoration, and honour, Father, Son, and Holy Spirit.

(Ephrem of Edessa, *The Life of St Mary the Harlot*)

READING: MATTHEW 26:36–41

³⁶ Then Jesus went with them to a place called Gethsemane, and he said to his disciples, "Sit here, while I go over there and pray." ³⁷ And taking with him Peter and the two sons of Zebedee, he began to be sorrowful and troubled. ³⁸ Then he said to them, "My soul is very sorrowful, even to death; remain here, and watch with me." ³⁹ And going a little farther he fell on his face and prayed, saying, "My Father, if it be possible, let this cup pass from me; nevertheless, not as I will, but as you will." ⁴⁰ And he came to the disciples and found them sleeping. And he said to Peter, "So, could you not watch with me one hour? ⁴¹ Watch and pray that you may not enter into temptation. The spirit indeed is willing, but the flesh is weak."

MEDITATION:

Christ himself … said that his soul was troubled unto death … He did this … to show us that … [his soul was] unequal to the task without the strength of Spirit.

(Tertullian, *Flight in Time of Persecution* 8.1)

READING: MARK 14:43–50

⁴³ And immediately, while he was still speaking, Judas came, one of the twelve, and with him a crowd with swords

and clubs, from the chief priests and the scribes and the elders. [44] Now the betrayer had given them a sign, saying, "The one I will kiss is the man. Seize him and lead him away under guard." [45] And when he came, he went up to him at once and said, "Rabbi!" And he kissed him. [46] And they laid hands on him and seized him. [47] But one of those who stood by drew his sword and struck the servant of the high priest and cut off his ear. [48] And Jesus said to them, "Have you come out as against a robber, with swords and clubs to capture me? [49] Day after day I was with you in the temple teaching, and you did not seize me. But let the Scriptures be fulfilled." [50] And they all left him and fled.

MEDITATION:

In this act is shown the apostles' frailty. In the first ardour of their faith they had promised to die with him, but in their fear, they forgot their promise and fled. The same we may see in those who undertake to do great things for the love of God, but fail to fulfil what they undertake. They ought not to despair, but be renewed with the apostles, and recover themselves by repentance.

(Remigius, cited in *Catena aurea*)

NOTES

NOTES

THURSDAY

⁶ All we like sheep have gone astray; we have turned—every one—to his own way; and the Lord has laid on him the iniquity of us all. ⁷ He was oppressed, and he was afflicted, yet he opened not his mouth; like a lamb that is led to the slaughter, and like a sheep that before its shearers is silent, so he opened not his mouth.

MEDITATION:

[Jesus] is called a Sheep, not a senseless one, but that which cleanses the world from sin by its precious blood, and when led before its shearers knows when to be silent. This

Sheep again is called a Shepherd, who says: "I am the good shepherd." [He is] a Sheep because of his human nature, a Shepherd because of the lovingkindness of his Godhead.

(Cyril of Jerusalem, *Catechesis* 10.3)

READING: MATTHEW 27:11–14

[11] Now Jesus stood before the governor, and the governor asked him, "Are you the King of the Jews?" Jesus said, "You have said so." [12] But when he was accused by the chief priests and elders, he gave no answer. [13] Then Pilate said to him, "Do you not hear how many things they testify against you?" [14] But he gave him no answer, not even to a single charge, so that the governor was greatly amazed.

MEDITATION:

Jesus is at all times assailed by false witnesses, and while wickedness remains in the world, [he] is ever exposed to accusation. And yet even now he continues silent before these things, and makes no audible answer, but places his defence in the lives of his genuine disciples.

(Origen, *Against Celsus* Preface.3)

READING: 1 PETER 2:21–25

[21] For to this you have been called, because Christ also

suffered for you, leaving you an example, so that you might follow in his steps. ²² He committed no sin, neither was deceit found in his mouth. ²³ When he was reviled, he did not revile in return; when he suffered, he did not threaten, but continued entrusting himself to him who judges justly. ²⁴ He himself bore our sins in his body on the tree, that we might die to sin and live to righteousness. By his wounds you have been healed. ²⁵ For you were straying like sheep, but have now returned to the Shepherd and Overseer of your souls.

MEDITATION:

In everything which concerns the Lord we find lessons in humility. … He did not make use of the marvellous power which he possessed to resist any of those who attacked him, but, as if yielding to superior force, he allowed temporal authority to exercise the power proper to it. He was brought before the High Priest as though a criminal and then led to the governor. He bore calumnies in silence and submitted to his sentence, although he could have refuted the false witnesses. He was spat upon by slaves and the vilest menials. He delivered himself up to death, the most shameful death known to men. Thus, from his birth to the end of his life, he experienced all the exigencies which befall mankind, and, after displaying humility to such a degree, he manifested his glory, associating with himself in glory those who had shared his disgrace.

(Basil, *Homily 20, Of Humility*)

NOTES

NOTES

GOOD FRIDAY

⁸ And they heard the sound of the Lord God walking in the garden in the cool of the day, and the man and his wife hid themselves from the presence of the Lord God among the trees of the garden. ⁹ But the Lord God called to the man and said to him, "Where are you?" ¹⁰ And he said, "I heard the sound of you in the garden, and I was afraid, because I was naked, and I hid myself." ¹¹ He said, "Who told you that you were naked? Have you eaten of the tree of which I commanded you not to eat?" ¹² The man said, "The woman whom you gave to be with me, she gave me fruit of the tree, and I ate." ¹³ Then the Lord God said to the woman, "What is this that you have done?" The woman

said, "The serpent deceived me, and I ate." [14] The Lord God said to the serpent,

> "Because you have done this, cursed are you above all livestock and above all beasts of the field; on your belly you shall go, and dust you shall eat all the days of your life. [15] I will put enmity between you and the woman, and between your offspring and her offspring; he shall bruise your head, and you shall bruise his heel."

MEDITATION:

From the tree came sin, and until the Tree sin lasted.

(Cyril of Jerusalem, *Catechesis* 13.19)

READING: 1 PETER 3:18–22

[18] For Christ also suffered once for sins, the righteous for the unrighteous, that he might bring us to God, being put to death in the flesh but made alive in the spirit, [19] in which he went and proclaimed to the spirits in prison, [20] because they formerly did not obey, when God's patience waited in the days of Noah, while the ark was being prepared, in which a few, that is, eight persons, were brought safely through water. [21] Baptism, which corresponds to this, now saves you, not as a removal of dirt from the body but as an appeal to God for a good conscience, through the

resurrection of Jesus Christ, [22] who has gone into heaven and is at the right hand of God, with angels, authorities, and powers having been subjected to him.

MEDITATION:

Instead of hating us and rejecting us and remembering our wickednesses against us, God showed how long-suffering he is. He bore with us, and in pity he took our sins upon himself and gave his own Son as a ransom for us—the Holy for the wicked, the Sinless for sinners, the Just for the unjust, the Incourruptible for the corruptible, the Immortal for the mortal. For was there, indeed, anything except his righteousness that could have availed to cover our sins? In whom could we, in our lawlessness and ungodliness, have been made holy, but in the Son of God alone? O sweet exchange! O unsearchable working! O benefits unhoped for!—that the wickedness of multitudes should thus be hidden in the One righteous, and the righteousness of One should justify the countless wicked!

(*Letter to Diognetus* 9.2–5)

READING: ROMANS 10:9

[9] If you confess with your mouth that Jesus is Lord and believe in your heart that God raised him from the dead, you will be saved.

MEDITATION:

Eternal happiness is obtained completely and solely by believing that God raised Jesus from the dead, by confessing that he is Lord.

(Hilary, *On the Trinity* 10.70)

NOTES

NOTES

SATURDAY

[19] For in him all the fullness of God was pleased to dwell, [20] and through him to reconcile to himself all things, whether on earth or in heaven, making peace by the blood of his cross.

[21] And you, who once were alienated and hostile in mind, doing evil deeds, [22] he has now reconciled in his body of flesh by his death, in order to present you holy and blameless and above reproach before him, [23] if indeed you continue in the faith, stable and steadfast, not shifting from the hope of the gospel that you heard, which has been proclaimed in all creation under heaven, and of which I, Paul, became a minister.

MEDITATION:

The cross [of Christ] destroyed the enmity of God towards humanity, brought about reconciliation, ... associated human beings with angels, pulled down the citadel of death, hamstrung the force of the devil, extinguished the power of sin, delivered the world from error, brought back the truth, expelled the demons, ... implanted virtue, and founded the Church. ... The cross has broken our bonds, it rendered the prison of death powerless, it demonstrated the love of God. ... The cross opened Paradise.

(John Chrysostom, *Sermon on Matthew* 26:29)

READING: ROMANS 6:1–5

¹ What shall we say then? Are we to continue in sin that grace may abound? ² By no means! How can we who died to sin still live in it? ³ Do you not know that all of us who have been baptized into Christ Jesus were baptized into his death? ⁴ We were buried therefore with him by baptism into death, in order that, just as Christ was raised from the dead by the glory of the Father, we too might walk in newness of life. ⁵ For if we have been united with him in a death like his, we shall certainly be united with him in a resurrection like his.

MEDITATION:

Whenever we are about to baptize, we proclaim the sacred and awe-inspiring words of the [Nicene] Creed, … "I believe in the resurrection of the dead," and on the basis of this faith we are baptized. After making this profession along with the others, we then descend into the font … This was the basis for your baptism, that you believe in the resurrection of the dead body, that it does not remain dead … Indeed, to be baptized by sinking down and rising again is a symbol of the descent into hell and the ascent from there. That is why Paul calls a baptism a burial, saying: "We were buried therefore with him by baptism into death [Romans 6:4]." In this way he makes the future event (I mean the resurrection of bodies) more believable. The removal of sins is a much greater thing than the resurrection of the body.

(John Chrysostom, *Homily* 40)

READING: COLOSSIANS 2:9–15

⁹ For in him the whole fullness of deity dwells bodily, ¹⁰ and you have been filled in him, who is the head of all rule and authority. ¹¹ In him also you were circumcised with a circumcision made without hands, by putting off the body of the flesh, by the circumcision of Christ, ¹² having been buried with him in baptism, in which you were

also raised with him through faith in the powerful working of God, who raised him from the dead. [13] And you, who were dead in your trespasses and the uncircumcision of your flesh, God made alive together with him, having forgiven us all our trespasses, [14] by canceling the record of debt that stood against us with its legal demands. This he set aside, nailing it to the cross. [15] He disarmed the rulers and authorities and put them to open shame, by triumphing over them in him.

MEDITATION:

It is in that faith [that Christ has triumphed over death] that we approach him and are baptized, because we wish to share from now on in his death, in the hope of sharing in those same good things, namely, to rise from the dead in the same manner that he has risen. For that reason, when I am baptized, by immersing my head, it is the death of the Lord Christ that I receive, and his burial which I wish to take upon myself. And there truly I already confess the resurrection of our Lord whilst in raising my head as a kind of figure, I perceive myself to be already raised.

(Theodore of Mopsuestia, *Catechetical Homily* 14.5)

NOTES

NOTES

EASTER SUNDAY

READING: PSALM 98:1–6

[1] Oh sing to the Lord a new song, for he has done marvelous things! His right hand and his holy arm have worked salvation for him. [2] The Lord has made known his salvation; he has revealed his righteousness in the sight of the nations. [3] He has remembered his steadfast love and faithfulness to the house of Israel. All the ends of the earth have seen the salvation of our God.

[4] Make a joyful noise to the Lord, all the earth; break forth into joyous song and sing praises! [5] Sing praises to the Lord with the lyre, with the lyre and the sound of melody! [6] With trumpets and the sound of the horn make a joyful noise before the King, the Lord!

READING: REVELATION 5

¹ Then I saw in the right hand of him who was seated on the throne a scroll written within and on the back, sealed with seven seals. ² And I saw a mighty angel proclaiming with a loud voice, "Who is worthy to open the scroll and break its seals?" ³ And no one in heaven or on earth or under the earth was able to open the scroll or to look into it, ⁴ and I began to weep loudly because no one was found worthy to open the scroll or to look into it. ⁵ And one of the elders said to me, "Weep no more; behold, the Lion of the tribe of Judah, the Root of David, has conquered, so that he can open the scroll and its seven seals."

⁶ And between the throne and the four living creatures and among the elders I saw a Lamb standing, as though it had been slain, with seven horns and with seven eyes, which are the seven spirits of God sent out into all the earth. ⁷ And he went and took the scroll from the right hand of him who was seated on the throne. ⁸ And when he had taken the scroll, the four living creatures and the twenty-four elders fell down before the Lamb, each holding a harp, and golden bowls full of incense, which are the prayers of the saints. ⁹ And they sang a new song, saying,

"Worthy are you to take the scroll and to open its seals,
for you were slain, and by your blood you ransomed
people for God from every tribe and language and

people and nation, [10] and you have made them a kingdom and priests to our God, and they shall reign on the earth."

[11] Then I looked, and I heard around the throne and the living creatures and the elders the voice of many angels, numbering myriads of myriads and thousands of thousands, [12] saying with a loud voice,

> "Worthy is the Lamb who was slain, to receive power and wealth and wisdom and might and honor and glory and blessing!"

[13] And I heard every creature in heaven and on earth and under the earth and in the sea, and all that is in them, saying,

> "To him who sits on the throne and to the Lamb be blessing and honor and glory and might forever and ever!"

[14] And the four living creatures said, "Amen!" and the elders fell down and worshiped.

READING: HEBREWS 13:20–21

[20] Now may the God of peace who brought again from

the dead our Lord Jesus, the great shepherd of the sheep, by the blood of the eternal covenant, [21] equip you with everything good that you may do his will, working in us that which is pleasing in his sight, through Jesus Christ, to whom be glory forever and ever. Amen.

MEDITATION:

> The day of resurrection!
> Earth, tell it out abroad;
> The Passover of gladness,
> The Passover of God.
> From death to life eternal,
> From earth unto the sky,
> Our Christ hath brought us over,
> With hymns of victory.
>
> Our hearts be pure from evil,
> That we may see aright
> The Lord in rays eternal
> Of resurrection light;
> And listening to his accents,
> May hear, so calm and plain,
> His own "All hail!" and, hearing,
> May raise the victor strain.
>
> Now let the heavens be joyful!

Michael A.G. Haykin

Let earth the song begin!
Let the round world keep triumph,
And all that is therein!
Let all things seen and unseen
Their notes in gladness blend,
For Christ the Lord hath risen,
Our joy that hath no end.

(John of Damascus)

NOTES

NOTES

GLOSSARY OF
AUTHORS

Athanasius of Alexandria (ca.299–373) was born and raised in Alexandria in a Christian home. He became the secretary to Alexander, the bishop of Alexandria, with whom he attended the Council of Nicaea (325). In 328, Athanasius succeeded Alexander as bishop. His life and ministry were devoted to the defence of the deity of Christ.

Augustine of Hippo (354–430) is one of the most important theologians in Christian history. Most of his early life are well known as it was recorded in his *Confessions* (397–401). Augustine came to faith in the summer of 386 in a garden in Milan. After his baptism in 387, Augustine moved back to North Africa, and in 395, he was elected bishop of Hippo, where Augustine ministered till his death. In addition to the *Confessions*, he was a prolific writer and wrote a number of remarkable works, including *On the Trinity* and *The City of God*.

Basil of Caesarea (330–379) was born to a Christian family in Cappadocia. He received his education in rhetoric in Cappadocia, Constantinople, and Athens. According to his brother Gregory of Nyssa (ca.335–ca.395), after Basil returned home, a conversation with his elder sister Macrina (ca.329–379) led to his conversion. As a bishop, Basil defended Trinitarian orthodoxy. Basil's most important work was his *On the Holy Spirit*, in which Basil defended the divinity of the Holy Spirit.

Catena aurea is an anthology of the works of the Greek and Latin authors of the Ancient Church drawn up by Thomas Aquinas (1225–1274).

John Chrysostom (ca.347–407), who was born in Antioch, was the archbishop of Constantinople, and became best known for his preaching. The epithet *Chrysostomos* means "golden-mouthed" in Greek, which denotes John's reputation as an orator.

Cyril of Jerusalem (ca.313–386) became the bishop of Jerusalem around 349. The most important surviving work of Cyril is a series of catechetical instructions delivered to new converts who were about to receive baptism.

Ephrem of Edessa (ca.306–373) was born in the city of Nisibis (modern Nusaybin, Turkey). Ephrem was a genius at the composition of hymns and poetry.

Hilary of Poitiers (ca.310–ca.367) was one of the most significant Latin-speaking theologians. Hilary wrote various biblical commentaries and a book on the Trinity.

John of Damascus (ca.675/676–749), or Yanah ibn Masur, was the earliest Christian apologist who responded to Islam. John was born in Damascus when it was the capital of the Arabic empire. John's *Fountain of Knowledge* is considered the first systematic theology textbook, which has greatly influenced Eastern Orthodoxy.

The Letter to Diognetus (ca.175) was written by an unknown author to a pagan friend by the name of Diognetus in which he explained to his friend what Christians believe and why they love each other the way that they do.

Macarius (fl.360–400) was a Syriac-speaking Christian was also fluent in Greek and was a spiritual mentor in Christian communities on the border of the Roman and Persian Empires. His sermons are some of the most valuable works of spirituality of the late fourth century.

Origen of Alexandria (ca.185–254) was a biblical exegete and theologian. Born in Egypt, Origen was raised in a Christian home. His father Leonidas was martyred in 202. Origen went on to become a celebrated theologian and apologist. During the persecution of Decius in 250, Origen was imprisoned and tortured, and subsequently died as a result.

Remigius of Reims (ca.437–533) was born at Cerny-en-Laonnois, in what is now Picardy in today's France. Due to his intellectual ability, Remigius was elected Bishop of Reims at age 21. Remigius was instrumental in bringing the gospel to the Franks.

Rufinus of Aquileia (ca.345–411) was a monk, historian, and theologian. He is remembered as the translator of Greek patristic books, especially the works of Origen.

Tertullian of Carthage (fl.190–220) was the first Latin-speaking theologian. Born in North Africa, he came to Christ when he was an adult. He was a prolific writer and is remembered for coining the term "Trinity."

Theodore of Mopsuestia (ca.350–428) was a Syrian theologian who was born in Antioch and came to be regarded as one of the greatest biblical interpreters of his time.

Theodulf of Orléans (750–821) was a poet and one of the leading theologians of the Frankish Empire.

Timothy of Baghdad (727–823) was born into a Christian home in Iran and in 780 he became the leading bishop of the East Syrian Church, a church that reached from the Middle East to China.

Date Completed	Name